Crossing Over From Death to Eternal Life
A True Story

Steve Harris

Crossing Over From Death to Eternal Life
A True Story

Second Impression
First Published in English in 2008

Published by Global Influencers
PO Box 308, Morningside QLD 4170, Australia
www.globalinfluencers.org
Copyright © 2008, 2021 by Steve Harris and Outpouring Ministries
All rights reserved

978-0-6450343-5-6 (Paperback)
978-0-6450343-2-5 (eBook)

This book or parts thereof may not be reproduced in any form, stored in a retrieval system, or transmitted in any form by any means - electronic, mechanical, photocopy, recording, or otherwise - without prior written permission of the publisher, except as provided by Australian copyright law.

Bible Versions Used

All Scripture quotations are taken from the Holy Bible, New International Version®, NIV®. Copyright © 1973, 1978, 1984, 2011 by Biblica, Inc.™ Used by permission of Zondervan. All rights reserved worldwide. www.zondervan.com

Foreword

Having crossed over from death to life,
I am, in a very real sense, a resurrected man.
I was involved in a serious car accident
that took the life from my body and sent
my spirit on a journey to the edge of eternity.

It is only by the grace of God, expressed through
the love and prayers of my grandmother,
that my spirit and soul were able to return
to my body, and that I am here today
to tell you the story of what happened.

This book is lovingly dedicated
to the memory and legacy
of my grandmother.

Crossing Over From Death to Eternal Life

A True Story

John 5:24-25
"I tell you the truth, whoever hears My word
and believes him who sent Me
has eternal life and will not be condemned;
he has crossed over from death to life.

I tell you the truth, a time is coming and has now come when the dead will hear the voice of the Son of God and those who hear will live."

I grew up in a family where no-one practiced any kind of faith or belief in God. My grandmother was the exception. From the moment that my mother was carrying me in her womb, my grandmother prayed to God on my behalf. I found out much later that she had promised God that if he would give her a grandson, then she would dedicate that grandson to Him.

And so, when I was born, that's exactly what she did. And she never stopped praying for me each and every day of her life.

I have no doubt that it was my grandmother's prayers that saved my life more than once. I know that it was largely her prayers that stopped my life from being cut short on the eve of my 24th birthday.

God Speaks

In spite of my non-religious and non-spiritual upbringing, I had a profound experience of God when I was just 10 years old.

The experience began in the middle of the night, and it began with a sound. I was captivated by the sound. It was musical - it sounded like voices and instruments mixed. It was one note, and many. It had dimensions to it that were simply not like any earthly sound. It was the most unique and beautiful sound I had ever heard. It contained beautiful words of an unknown language that were being spoken and sung at the same time. It was just wonderful.

I was drawn to the sound, and the sound also drew me - upwards, into a beautiful place that was filled with glorious, radiant light. I was met by a man who was clothed in brilliant white from head to toe. I didn't know then, but do know now, that it was Jesus. He spoke to me and said, "Steve, all of creation flows from this sound!"

(In the beginning was the *Word* ... God *spoke* and said, 'Let there be light ... ' **John 1:1, Genesis 1:3**). This beautiful sound that I had heard was the voice of God, creating and sustaining all things by *speaking* and *singing* over His creation.

"The LORD your God is with you, he is mighty to save. He will take great delight in you, he will quiet you with his love, he will rejoice over you with singing." (**Zephaniah 3:17** and also see **Hebrews 1:3**)

I was absolutely amazed, and also curious. I asked Him, 'What is the secret? Can *I* make this sound?' He just smiled at me ! Then, the experience began to fade (but not the sound).

When the experience began to fade, I felt so sad! I wanted to stay in that beautiful place for ever. I even tried to write down the music that I had just heard. It was impossible of course – but I tried. And I can still remember the character and beauty of that wonderful sound to this day.

God must have imparted something to me during that Heavenly experience because it was just a few days later that I started playing the piano by ear, with no formal training at all. I began playing in bands at age 14 and went on from there to play the keyboards on numerous recordings (including gold albums) and also to perform live in many different countries.

Wherever I went, people always commented that there was something 'different' about the way that I played the keyboards. As I think about those days, I feel certain that I must have carried the touch from that Heavenly encounter into my music.

After quite a few years of involvement in many popular rock bands, I became extremely disillusioned with the rock scene.

I moved into Latin, jazz, funk, reggae, and African music, and enjoyed not only the music but also the African, South American, Caribbean, indigenous Australian, Maori, and Melanesian cultures.

But - although we had the rhythm, we had the joy, we made people dance, clap, sing, and forget about their troubles for a while; and even sang songs about God, the lyrics that we were singing just did not reconcile with the life style that we were living. I began to ask questions.

I began to question the people around me who seemed to have their lives all figured out. I would ask them serious questions about this life and the next – and then I would quickly find that many who seemed so self-assured were just as uncertain and insecure as I was when it came to the eternal questions.

The Turning Point

Two musician friends and I were in a small car, driving down the highway from one musical engagement to the next. It was 10 minutes to midnight, on the eve of my 24th birthday. It's difficult to describe in words what happened next.

Wham. Utter darkness. Sirens were screaming. There was an unrecognisable mass of blood, torn flesh, and broken bones where my best friend – who was driving at the moment of impact – should have been.

These were the sights and sounds of a horrific head-on car accident. My best friend was driving and one of the female singers from our band was sitting in the back seat. I was the front seat passenger. I was not aware of what had happened until I regained consciousness after the accident.

It all happened so quickly. On the night of the accident, we were all completely sober – which is one of the reasons that we managed to survive.

The other reason is that we were travelling at 90 kilometres per hour (just under 60 miles per hour) - 20 kilometres under the speed limit.

By contrast, the other vehicle – a heavy duty pickup truck – was being driven by a man whose blood alcohol level was 6 times above the legal limit.

When our vehicles collided, he was travelling at 160 kilometres per hour (100 miles per hour) and he was travelling north on the southbound lanes of the freeway – placing himself on a certain collision course with any oncoming traffic. It was a foggy night and he had forgotten to switch on his headlights - so we had no chance at all of seeing him before the moment of impact.

The driver of our car was so badly injured, he remained in a coma for 6 months. The rear seat passenger sustained multiple fractures, including a broken pelvis, and serious lacerations. Such was the force of the impact, the car body was severely compressed, like an accordion, and as a result, my head went straight through the front windscreen and shattered it.

My eyes and ears were filled with tiny slivers of windscreen glass, some of which remained embedded for more than 3 years.

I cracked my skull and still have a lump on it today as a reminder of the accident. My right side was also injured and I still have a slight limp to this day.

Every section of the car with the exception of the area surrounding the front passenger seat (the location where I had been sitting) was completely shattered and mutilated.

Photographs taken at the scene revealed something miraculous. It appeared as though a giant hand had shielded that portion of the car, and therefore my body, from more serious harm.

This was an extremely serious accident, and in spite of the miraculous protection, I was so severely concussed and traumatised that I have only the vaguest recollections of the three years of my life that followed it.

However, the events leading up to the accident, and the amazing events that occurred at the moment of impact, can never be forgotten.

Warned Through a Dream

Three days **before** the accident I had a vivid dream which literally **was** the accident, down to the minutest of details - the make, model and license plate number of the vehicle that impacted ours; the appearance of the driver; the extent of his injuries; the position in which his vehicle came to rest; the flames pouring out of his engine; the conversations with the ambulance team; and so on.

I woke up from that dream, absolutely terrified. The entire bed was literally soaked with sweat.

I KNEW that this dream was a warning of something real that was going to happen.

The only question was, when?

The Moment of Impact

Going back to the moment of impact - the combined velocity of our car and the truck that hit us was 250 kilometres per hour (160 miles per hour). We had no chance of preparing ourselves for the impact, let alone even seeing the approaching vehicle.
My head went straight through the front windscreen and shattered it.

The impact was so strong and so sudden, it could have ended my life permanently right there and then. Remember that the driver of our car ended up in a coma for six months, fighting for his life.

From the point of view of my conscious mind, however, I was still sitting in a car, travelling down the highway to play music, as I had done hundreds of times before.

As you will see, it is clear from the events that followed, that my spirit left my body and if not for the grace of God my life would have been over.

That's not the 24th birthday present that I would have chosen for myself.

Another World

At the moment of physical death, the spirit and soul separate from the body, never to be joined again. During the experience that followed the accident, for all intents and purposes, I WAS dead.

That is, my spirit had separated itself from my body. Fortunately, because of the grace of God, the separation of spirit and body in my case was not yet permanent.

This is what happened next.

While my body lay dead in the front seat of the car, my spirit and soul were lifted out of my body and propelled upwards through a tight, winding tunnel. The diameter of the tunnel was tight, with the face of it very close to me as I travelled upwards.

The sides of the tunnel seemed to be woven or ribbed, and the tunnel was embedded with red lights that looked like eyes.

It was a deeply unsettling experience.

Remember, I had been sitting in a car and I had no idea that I had been in an accident. It was the middle of the night and I had been travelling down Highway One.

Now, I was in a different and completely unfamiliar place, where time seemed to be standing still, and I had absolutely no idea how I had arrived there.

Eventually the upward journey ceased. I looked around and found that I was now standing in the middle of a large, flat, white space, still unfamiliar, but not unpleasant.

The ground was white and the sky was dull white. The ground and sky were featureless and the horizon seemed far away. Throughout the entire expanse, there was very little variation in appearance.

After my eyes had adjusted to my new surroundings, I noticed what appeared to be city lights at the distant edges of the vast white expanse. The lights appeared to be twinkling and I wondered what they could be. Could they be the lights of a city?

I still felt very strange and a little bit unsettled, but I started to reason that if I could get to the 'city lights' I might be able to find out where I was.

I was still looking around, and trying to make sense of these strange vistas, when suddenly I was approached by a tall, white haired elderly man, who was dressed entirely in black, from head to toe.

He seemed to just 'appear', very suddenly, out of nowhere. He embraced me in a friendly manner and said, 'Welcome, Steve, we've been waiting for you'... and for a moment, I felt special. I felt as though somehow, this weird excursion must have been pre – arranged, because someone was waiting for me.

My new 'friend' embraced my shoulders with a firm grip and began walking with me and chatting to me.

He seemed friendly enough and he seemed to know his way around, and so I felt slightly happier, and even a little bit excited.

At an earlier stage of my life, I had been involved in transcendental meditation and I'd always longed for out-of-body experiences. I remember having the thought that perhaps this was an out-of-body experience. Sure enough, although I didn't know it, my spirit had actually left my body - but not in a pre-meditated way at all.

I began to ask him where we were, and where we were going, but he kept brushing off my questions and continued with his conversation.

He was speaking a lot but, after the first 'welcoming' phrase, I found that I couldn't actually understand any of his words.

After what seemed to be about 5 or 10 minutes of walking, the distant 'city lights' were becoming much nearer and brighter. Again, I asked where we were and where we were going.

Again, he interrupted me, but I also noticed a subtle change in my 'friend's' behaviour. His firm grip on my shoulders had become much stronger, and his smile had become less friendly. We were also beginning to walk much more quickly.

He told me not to worry about where we were going, and that I would soon see for myself. And then, he began to speak very quickly again and I couldn't understand another word.

I began to panic, and asked again, more forcefully this time, where we were and where were we going. I tried to break away from his grip but could not.

This time, my guide became very angry and snapped at me to keep quiet. His grip became stronger again. By now, I was starting to feel really scared and concerned for my wellbeing.
I quickly made a decision within myself that I would dig my heels into the ground, break the momentum of our journey, and refuse to go any further until my guide had explained to me exactly who he was and exactly where he was taking me.

I did manage to dig my heels into the ground, and I did manage to break the momentum, and we did stop for a moment.

I lifted up my face and began to say the words "I'm not going any further until you tell me … "

But … as I looked up into what had been a human face, I found that I was now confronted with a hideous demonic face.
The arms that had embraced my shoulders were now revealed as black ribbed wings with sharp claws attached to them.

The 'person' was revealing itself for what it was – a horrible demonic creature that was trying to end my life, by forcing me into a terrible journey from which there could be no return.
You see, we had suddenly reached the edge of the 'whiteness'. It was now very clear that what had appeared to be city lights from a distance were not city lights at all.

They were flames.

I stood on the very edge of a huge fiery landscape, full of pits, foul smoke, terrible smells and sounds. And I could see people, with twisted bodies and broken limbs, sitting amongst the flames, screaming.

My 'guide' was now laughing hideously and forcefully attempting to throw me over the edge, to my eternal doom.

I was frozen with fear, terrified, and not knowing what to do. But just as he was about to do throw me over the edge, something awakened deep inside of me.

There was a dim spark of consciousness, something telling me that this wasn't right, that things didn't have to be this way.

I threw back my head and screamed 'Nooooo….' … and as soon as I did that, I heard a loud 'snap' like a tight bowstring being released and there was a very strong pull on the back of my neck as if I were attached to a giant elastic band … I was forcibly pulled away from that place and all the way back, across the white plain, and down through the tunnel.

Ecclesiastes Chapter 12, Verse 6, says –
Remember Him, before the silver cord is severed …

The "silver cord" referred to here is a spiritual connector that joins our body and spirit together. It is severed at the time of death. My 'silver cord' was stretched to the absolute limits of its breaking point.

Remember I had a completely non-religious and non-spiritual upbringing and I had no concept of heaven or hell. My experience was not based upon any preconceived ideas or on things I had been taught as a child.

The things that I saw are real. Whether I believed in it or not, I was standing on the edge of a place called Hell. I was headed to an awful eternity in a place that was terrible beyond imagining, and it was filled with people who probably didn't believe in it either, until they found themselves there.

Back To Earth

It was at this precise moment that I awoke, in the car, with a strong breeze blowing on my face. My first thought was that there shouldn't have been any breeze; I was in a car, travelling with my friends to play music.

Then I realised that we were stopped, that there was no windscreen, which is why I could feel the breeze.

(Wham. Utter darkness. Sirens were screaming. There was an unrecognisable mass of blood, torn flesh, and broken bones where my best friend – who was driving at the moment of impact – should have been.)

In spite of my own injuries, I tried to revive my friend, even though because of his horrific injuries he was not even recognisable as a human being. Then, everything else began to unfold exactly as it had been revealed to me in my dream of a few nights earlier.

The ambulance team that attended the accident scene found me wandering around in the bushes by the side of the road. They asked "Who are you?" They were incredulous when I told them that I had been the front seat passenger of that wrecked car.

I wonder what they would have thought if I'd tried to tell them what had just happened to my soul.

I rode in the back of the ambulance and I was treated in hospital. The nursing staff began to scrub my eyes even though they were full of glass slivers. I was screaming with the pain yet they kept scrubbing.
It's a miracle that I did not sustain permanent retinal damage and that I can see well today. I discharged myself that night from the hospital because I was terrified wondering what else could happen if I stayed.

A friend drove me home and I spent eight weeks in bed trying to recover from the accident.

The right side of my face and head were swollen and disfigured, and my general appearance due to my injuries was so bad that the rest of my housemates actually moved out! It took years to recover from the trauma of these experiences.

There are two things that saved me from losing my life during this out of body experience. The first thing was the faithful prayers of my grandmother. A few years after this experience, she told me how she had prayed for me every morning, noon, and evening from the moment that I was conceived.

Every day, she would pray that God would save my soul from hell and that I would give my life to Christ.

If anyone ever tells you that they are praying for you, you should be very grateful to them, as their prayers may just save your life one day.

The second thing that saved my life is the dream that I had just a few days before the accident.

Because of the dream, the memory of the accident was already implanted in my subconscious mind before the accident had occurred.

That memory gave me just enough consciousness of what was really happening, to be able to resist during the life and death struggle with a demonic being, who had been assigned to end my life by throwing my soul into the fires of hell.

The vision that I had at 10 years old, and the experience that I had on my 24th birthday, could not have been more different. One was beautiful, a tiny glimpse into the eternal dwelling place of a loving God.

The other was so bad, a frightening experience of a place ruled by demons and filled with people who had chosen to live separately from God and who ultimately had chosen to reject Him.

God's love is so great – and His mercy endures forever. He doesn't want anyone to be separated from Him. It's the choices that we make that separate us from Him.

Hell is the domain of demons. It is not designed for human beings. We will only arrive there if we choose to reject our Creator's offer of eternal life. He made us, and He loves us with an everlasting love.

He wants us to spend eternity with Him, in that glorious place called Heaven, that He has prepared specially for us. He will forgive anything that we have done if we will change our way of thinking about God, ourselves, and others (repent), and receive His free offer of forgiveness.

We need to believe and trust in Him now, while we are living on the earth. We are His children, and His plans for us are good.

Yet we have an enemy – the devil - who wants to deceive us regarding God's good intentions towards us, and to end our lives before we have taken the opportunity to make our peace with God.

Today is the best day to make your peace with God if you haven't already done so. At the end of this booklet, you will find instructions on how to do that, and how to know with certainty exactly where you will spend eternity.

Seeking the God of Love

I had plenty of time to think in the weeks that followed the accident. The dream, the death experience, and the accident itself, played over and over in my mind.

Every time I closed my eyes to try to sleep, I would have to deal with a slow-motion replay of the moment of impact. Somehow my mind had recorded every detail and it just kept playing them over and over. I nearly lost my mind during the recovery period.

Yet, there were deeper questions that needed solving. Where had I gone? Had I died? How was I able to come back? How could my finite mind have a dream about a future event?

I'll never forget the day that the realisation hit me that there must be a God, and that He must love me, because He had warned me about the danger that my soul was in and He gave me a chance to come back, not just for my own sake, but so that I could tell my story all over the world and warn others about the eternal consequences of the choices that we make.

The day that I realised that there was a God Who loved me and cared about my life, I did something I'd never done before. I prayed to my Creator.

My first prayer went something like this:

"God, I don't know who You are, and I can't imagine why you would love me, but please, reveal yourself to me. Show me who You are. Show me all the different ways that people seek You. When I find out who You really are, I will dedicate my life to You, and I will live for You."

Within just a few days of my prayer, there was a knock on the door. I was invited to participate in a 6-month band tour of South East Asia.

I protested – "my injuries ... " – but ended up going anyway.

During the six months in Asia God moved supernaturally in my life and opened doors that allowed me to meet the high priests of almost every major world religion. I was taught the inner secrets and sacred teachings of all of them.
From the beginning of my life until now, I have always had a deep love and respect for all who sincerely seek to know God. But in spite of all the amazing experiences that I had during those six months in Asia, I did not find the God who loved me and Who had saved me from the fires of hell.

It was almost four years later that someone gave me a Bible. I started to read it. There were a few verses that really spoke to me and stirred something deep inside of me. I wondered if, in Jesus Christ, I had found the God of love. But I still didn't take the necessary steps to make my peace with Him.

The Moment Of Truth

It took four more years, and another supernatural encounter ... before I gave my life to Christ.

Once again, I had a dream. This time, in the dream, I was on my way to work. I boarded the usual morning train, and finished the journey at my usual stop. Suddenly, everything melted away, and I found myself standing in the desert.
A glorious bright light appeared in the sky, and a powerful voice spoke to me out of the light.

The voice said, "Steve, are you serious about following me, or are you just talking about it?" You see, He knew that I had been telling a few friends that I was thinking about becoming a Christian, because I wanted to know if they would still be my friends if I became one !

In the dream, I dropped to my knees because I **knew** Who was speaking to me from the middle of the light.

It was Jesus. On my knees, I said to Him, "LORD, You know that I need You, 24 hours a day, 7 days a week, for the rest of my life."

He responded and told me to go find the biggest church that I could find and to tell them the same thing that I had just told Him.

And so, I did. And just like that, I was born again, out of a life of darkness and uncertainty, and into a wonderful new life filled with the eternal love, mercy, grace, and peace of Jesus Christ.

From that moment, I had crossed over from a road that led to death, on to the road that leads to Eternal Life. **(John 5 : 24-25)**

Serving The Servant King

Within the first hour of my salvation, I laid down all of my musical gifts, right there at the foot of the cross of Jesus. I had to! Music had been my life, but I knew that from now on, my life would be different. There were to be no regrets and no looking back.

I told Him, "LORD, take it away! I don't want or need it any more !" But He didn't take it away. Instead, He increased the gift that was already on my life. He instructed me to take up the music and to use it in the ways that He would show me, and that as I played to Him in softness and simplicity, He would release His Presence and do great and mighty things. And this is exactly what has happened ever since.

There's no place I'd rather be, and nothing I'd rather do, than lead people into the glorious Presence of the God of Love through worship.

Also through worship, God has opened many miraculous doors. I have seen His glory; I have been with angels. I've had many more supernatural encounters – thankfully, of the good kind !

He has used me to lead thousands closer to His throne just by playing His song. He has empowered me to preach and teach, to go to the mission field, to the hospitals, and to the prisons.

As I have prayed for people all over the world, I have witnessed tens of thousands of healing miracles - blind eyes, deaf ears and mute mouths opened, the lame walking, shrivelled hands restored, cancer, tuberculosis and other life-threatening illnesses completely healed, as well as all kinds of supernatural signs and wonders.

Over and over again, I have been privileged to witness the greatest miracle of all, the **salvation** of thousands upon thousands of souls as I have shared the Gospel – the Heavenly Good News that Jesus came to share with us all. There is nothing more beautiful in this life than to be a channel of blessing to others, and to bring others into the knowledge of eternal life through Jesus Christ.

And I know that there is so much more to do for God in this life, and all for His Glory. May this story inspire you to give your life to Jesus, and if you already have, may you be inspired to do even greater exploits in His Name. Amen.

Crossing Over from Death to Life
Biblical References

Heaven and Hell are Real

John 14 : 2-6

In my Father's house are many rooms;
if it were not so, I would have told you.
I am going there to prepare a place for you.

And if I go and prepare a place for you,
I will come back and take you to be with me
that you also may be where I am.
You know the way to the place where I am going."
Thomas said to him, "Lord, we don't know
where you are going, so how can we know the way?"

Jesus answered,
"I Am the Way and the Truth and the Life.
No one comes to the Father except through Me."

Revelation 4:1-2
After these things I looked, and behold, a door standing open in heaven. And the first voice which I heard was like a trumpet speaking with me, saying, "Come up here, and I will show you things which must take place after this."

Immediately I was in the Spirit; and behold, a throne set in heaven, and One sat on the throne.

Luke 16 : 19-31
"There was a rich man who was dressed in purple and fine linen and lived in luxury every day.

At his gate was laid a beggar named Lazarus, covered with sores and longing to eat what fell from the rich man's table. Even the dogs came and licked his sores.

The time came when the beggar died and the angels carried him to Abraham's side. The rich man also died and was buried.

In hell, where he was in torment, he looked up and
saw Abraham far away, with Lazarus by his side.

So he called to him, 'Father Abraham,
have pity on me and send Lazarus to dip
the tip of his finger in water and cool my tongue,
because I am in agony in this fire.'

But Abraham replied, 'Son, remember that
in your lifetime you received your good things,
while Lazarus received bad things, but now
he is comforted here and you are in agony.

And besides all this, between us and you
a great chasm has been fixed, so that those
who want to go from here to you cannot,
nor can anyone cross over from there to us.'

He answered, 'Then I beg you, father,
send Lazarus to my father's house, for I have
five brothers. Let him warn them, so that
they will not also come to this place of torment.'

Abraham replied, 'They have Moses
and the Prophets; let them listen to them.'

'No, father Abraham,' he said, 'but if someone
from the dead goes to them, they will repent.'

He said to him, 'If they do not listen to Moses
and the Prophets, they will not be convinced
even if someone rises from the dead.'"

Luke 13 : 22-30

Then Jesus went through the towns and villages,
teaching as he made his way to Jerusalem.

Someone asked him,
"Lord, are only a few people going to be saved?"

He said to them, "Make every effort to enter
through the narrow door, because many, I tell you,
will try to enter and will not be able to.

Once the owner of the house gets up and
closes the door, you will stand outside knocking
and pleading, 'Sir, open the door for us.' "

But he will answer, 'I don't know you or where
you come from.' Then you will say, 'We ate
and drank with you, and you taught in our streets.'
"But he will reply, 'I don't know you or where you
come from. Away from me, all you evildoers!'
"There will be weeping there, and gnashing of teeth,
when you see Abraham, Isaac and Jacob
and all the prophets in the kingdom of God,
but you yourselves thrown out.

People will come from east and west and north
and south, and will take their places
at the feast in the kingdom of God.

Indeed there are those who are last who will
be first, and first who will be last."

The Speech and Songs of God

Genesis 1:3
And God said, "Let there be light,"
and there was light.

John 1:1
In the beginning was the Word, and the Word
was with God, and the Word was God.

Hebrews 1:3a
The Son is the radiance of God's glory
and the exact representation of his being,
sustaining all things by his powerful word.

No One Knows When or How ...

Ecclesiastes 8:8
No man has power over the wind to contain it;
so no one has power over the day of his death.

...except Jesus

Revelation 1:18
I am the Living One; I was dead,
and behold I am alive for ever and ever!
And I hold the keys of death and Hades.

John 14:6
Jesus answered,
"I am the way and the truth and the life.
No one comes to the Father except through me."

INVITATION TO MAKE YOUR PEACE WITH GOD

Dear Friend, it's possible that you have read this booklet because someone who loves you very much has given it to you. It's also possible that you have read this far, without knowing Jesus Christ as LORD, or without understanding that you need to make your peace with God.

If that is you, please read on, because I would like to explain to you how easy it is, and how wonderful it is, to receive Jesus Christ into your heart and into your life. He wants to give you the free gift of eternal life, and it is as easy as sincerely believing in Him and sincerely receiving Him.

Step 1 - Understand that God has a plan for your life – and it's a good plan

His plan for you involves the free gift of true love, peace, joy, and abundant and eternal life.

Jeremiah 29:11 (NIV)
"For I know the plans I have for you," declares the LORD, "plans to prosper you and not to harm you, plans to give you hope and a future".

Romans 5:1 (NIV)
*We have peace with God
through our LORD Jesus Christ.*

John 3:16 (NIV)
*For God so loved the world
that He gave His only begotten Son,
that whoever believes in Him
should not perish but have everlasting life.*

John 10:10 (NIV)
*I (Jesus) have come that they may have life,
and that they may have it more abundantly.*

Step 2 - Understand that your life choices have separated you from God

God created us in His own image, and He gave each of us the gift of free will and free choice.

Unfortunately, most of us did not understand or appreciate this gift, and the choices that we have made have taken us far from the path of divine destiny and eternal love that was meant just for us.

This has resulted in separation from God and from His wonderful plan for our life.

The Bible says in **Romans 3:23** :-
For all have sinned and fall short of the glory of God.

And in **Romans 6:23 (NIV)** we read :-
For the wages of sin is death, but the gift of God is eternal life in Christ Jesus our LORD.

Proverbs 14:12 (NIV) says :-
"There is a way that seems right to a man, but in the end it leads to death."

Isaiah 59:2 (NIV)
But your iniquities have separated you from your God; your sins have hidden his face from you, so that he will not hear.

Step 3 - Understand that God has made a Way back to Himself through the Cross of Calvary

God knew that many, in ignorance of the truth, would walk away from Him. And so, He provided a way for us to return to Him. He sent His one and only beloved Son, Jesus Christ to die on the Cross as a sacrifice for our sins and wrong doing.

Because of His sacrifice, we can have peace with God, if we are willing to repent (change our way of thinking about God, ourselves, and others) and to receive His free gift of salvation.

Not only did Jesus die in our place and pay the penalty for our sins, but He defeated the power of death and rose from the grave.

He now personally invites each of us to follow Him into eternal life and eternal glory.

Romans 5:8 (NIV)
But God demonstrates his own love for us in this:
While we were still sinners, Christ died for us.

Colossians 1:19-22 (NIV)
For God was pleased ... through Him (Jesus)
to reconcile to Himself all things, whether things on earth
or things in heaven, by making peace through his blood,
shed on the cross.

Once you were alienated from God and were enemies
in your minds because of your evil behavior.

But now he has reconciled you by Christ's physical body
through death to present you holy in his sight,
without blemish and free from accusation.

1 Timothy 2:5 (NIV)
For there is one God and one mediator
between God and men, the man Jesus Christ.

Step 4 - Trust and believe God, and make your own decision to receive Christ into your heart, TODAY.

If you have read this far, it is because God is speaking directly to you, and He is calling you to take your rightful place as a member of His eternal family.

This is the most important decision of your life, and it is a decision that will activate God's gift of eternal life within you as soon as you make it. The best time to make this decision is – today.

Hebrews 4:7 (NIV)
Today, if you hear his voice, do not harden your hearts.

Romans 10:9 (NIV)
*If you confess with your mouth, 'Jesus is LORD,'
and believe in your heart that God raised Him
from the dead, you will be saved.*

John 1:12 (NIV)
*Yet to all who received him,
to those who believed in his name,
He gave the right to become children of God.*

Step 5 – Pray – Talk to God – Tell Him that you have decided to come back to Him

Prayer is talking to God. Your first prayer is your first conversation with your Creator, and through it, if your heart is sincere, He is about to give you the gift of eternal life. All you have to do is ask Him for it. Prayer simply means "talking with God." You can speak to Him through prayer in the same way that you speak to a person.

Please pray the following prayer, with a sincere heart. There is no need to feel shy or hesitant. Your Creator God has been waiting and longing for you to have this exact conversation with Him, since the beginning of time.

"LORD Jesus, I know that I am a sinner and that I need Your forgiveness. Today I choose to repent - to change my way of thinking about You, myself, and others.

I believe that You died for my sins. I want to turn from my sins and live a life that is pleasing to you. I want to live according to Your plan for my life, and I need Your help to do that.

I now invite You to come into my heart and life. I want to trust and follow You as LORD and Savior. I ask and pray this in Jesus' Name. Amen."

If you prayed this prayer sincerely, the Bible assures you (in **Romans 10:13 (NIV)**) that:-

*Everyone who calls on the
Name of the LORD will be saved.*

And in **Ephesians 2:8-9 (NIV)**
we have this assurance :-

*For it is by grace you have been saved,
through faith - and this not from yourselves,
it is the gift of God - not by works,
so that no one can boast.*

Congratulations, and welcome to the family of God! Your life will never be the same again.

The Bible says that angels are rejoicing right now because of your decision.

Luke 15:10
"In the same way, I tell you, there is rejoicing in the presence of the angels of God over one sinner who repents."

Now, it's essential that you continue to walk in the pathway of your new life as a member of the family of God. The next page contains some helpful advice to help you to do that.

How to Walk With God

Here are some important steps that will help you to grow and become a strong Christian :-

1) Obtain a Bible and read it every day;

2) Seek out the friendship and fellowship of other Christians who are walking strongly with God;

3) Talk to God in prayer every day;

4) Tell others about your decision to follow Jesus;

5) Ask the person who gave you this booklet, or other Christians that you may know, if they can help you to find a good local church where you can spend time with committed Christians, who can help you to grow stronger in your faith.

6) Find out about water baptism
(God will seal you as His own);

7) Find out about the Baptism of the Holy Spirit *(God will fill you with His divine power to live a powerful, supernatural life)*. God bless you !

About the Author

Apostle Steve Harris has walked with Jesus since 1987. He has been blessed to worship with ministers such as Ron Kenoly and Pastor Benny Hinn.

He has taught the Word of God and preached the Gospel in many nations of the world, with salvation, healing, and miracles often accompanying the message.

As the founder of Outpouring Ministries (an organisation that exists to make a difference in a world full of desperate need), Steve has established mercy ministries in developing nations, constructing wells, computer and sewing schools, and establishing small to medium enterprises to permanently lift communities out of poverty.

He is also the founder of Global Influencers, a global community joined together in agape love and growing through the truth of God's Word and the fire of the Holy Spirit. Members are trained and equipped to walk in the fullness of the Gospel of the Kingdom, and to restore Kingdom culture from grassroots to government in the villages, cities, regions, and nations of the world.

Steve is commissioned through the Full Gospel Churches of Australia and ARC Global / H.I.M. He is the author of numerous books, and the composer of 3 worship CDs.

Worship CDs

www.globalinfluencers.org/resources
https://steveharris.hearnow.com
www.youtube.com/@steveharrisworship

Books

www.globalinfluencers.org/books

www.ingramcontent.com/pod-product-compliance
Lightning Source LLC
Chambersburg PA
CBHW032018290426
44109CB00013B/707